The Rev' Spiralizer

Diet Cookbook

(A Beginner's Guide):

The 22-day Top 60 Delicious and Mouth Watery Vegetable Pasta, Noodle, Salads and Side Dishes: Recipes to Help Reset Metabolism, Boost Energy and Lose Weight

By
DAVIS POWELL

Copyright © 2019 by: DAVIS POWELL

ISBN-13: 978-1-950772-45-2
ISBN-10: 1-950772-45-4

All Rights Reserved. No part of this publication may be reproduced in any form or by any means, including scanning, photocopying, or otherwise without prior written permission of the copyright holder.

Disclaimer:

The information provided in this book is designed to provide helpful information on the subjects discussed. The publisher and author are not responsible for any specific health or allergy needs that may require medical supervision and are not liable for any damages or negative consequences from any treatment, action, application or preparation, to any person reading or following the information in this book.

Table of Contents

INTRODUCTION 5
HOW YOU CAN BEST MAINTAIN YOUR SPIRALIZER 5
Vegetable that can give you the best result when spiralized 6
THE REV' SPIRALIZER COOKBOOK FOR A HEALTHIER YOU 8

Butternut Squash Rice, Sausage, Apple and Pecan Stuffing 8
Pumpkin Spice Sweet Potato Noodle Waffles (Gluten-Free) 10
Fall Harvest Butternut Squash Rice and Lentil Pilaf 11
Roasted Butternut Squash Noodles with Orange-Cranberry Sauce & Honey Roasted Pecans ... 13
Apple Tuna Salad Bell Pepper Sandwich 15
Spinach and Apple Noodle Salad with Pecans and Cranberries 17
Easy Apple Noodle & Rhubarb Crisps 18
Inspiralized Kale Waldorf salad 19
Maple Brussel Sprout & Ham Hash with Apple Noodles 21
Easy Apple Crisp with Peanut Butter Granola 23
Beet Noodles with Tomatoes, Feta and Bacon 24
Jalapeno-Citrus Golden Beet Noodle Salad with Crab, Avocado and Toasted Almonds ... 26
Beet Noodle, Pea and Arugula Salad with Lemon-Garlic Tahini Sauce 28
Raw Beet Noodle and Rainbow Chard Salad with Avocado-Ranch Dressing 30
Crunchy Miso Beet Rice with Spinach and Egg 32
Thyme Beet Risotto with Walnuts 34
Beet Noodle, Feta and Avocado Omelet 35
Roasted Beet Noodles with Pesto and Baby Kale 37
Mini Cheese Plate with Warm Beet Noodles 38
Quick Pickled Beets and Yellow Wax Beans with Feta and Chives 39
Candy Cane Beet Noodle and Arugula Quinoa Salad with Parmesan-Garlic Vinaigrette ... 40
Chilled Sweet and Sour Cucumber Noodles 42
Dan Noodles & Pickled Cucumber Salad 43
Spicy Moroccan Chickpeas with Beet Noodles 45
Sparkling Cider Glazed Roasted Beet Noodles with Crispy Shallots 47
Pesto Turkey & Beet Rice Lettuce Wraps 49
Roasted Orange & Beet Noodle Pasta with Honey Walnuts & Crispy Baked Kale 51

- Garlic Broccoli Noodles with Toasted Pine Nuts 53
- Spicy Tilapia and Black Radish Spaghetti with Cilantro-Jalapeno Avocado Tomato Sauce 55
- Spiral zed Garlic-Paprika Sweet Potato "Fries" 57
- Roasted Sweet Potato and Yam Noodles with Fennel, Charred Tomatoes, Olives and Pecorino 58
- Garlic Asia go Baked Spiralized Fries 60
- Spiralized Tzimmes for Rosh Hashanah 61
- Savoy Cabbage "Breakfast Burrito" with Sweet Potato Noodles 63
- Pesto Broccoli Sweet Potato Rice Casserole 64
- Garlic Sweet Potato Rice 66
- Butternut Squash Mac and Cheese 67
- Spicy Garlic Lump Crab Butternut Squash Pasta with Feta & Parsley 68
- Roasted Butternut Squash Noodles & Quinoa with Spiced Pumpkin Seeds, Dried Cranberries and Goat Cheese 69
- Roasted Butternut Squash Zucchini Pasta with Kale, Apricots and Wheat berries 71
- Zucchini Rice with Cranberries, Bacon, Goat Cheese and Walnuts with Maple-Dijon Dressing 73
- Greek Zucchini "Orzo" Salad 75
- Al Fresco Zucchini Pasta Salad 77
- Directions: 77
- Raw Coconut-Mango Zucchini Noodles with Cashews 78
- Thai Quinoa and Zucchini Noodle Salad 79
- Summer Zucchini Pasta Salad with Greek Yogurt-Herb Dressing 81
- Spiralized Sushi Bowl with Salmon Sashimi and Ginger Miso Dressing 83
- Basque Chicken with Red Potato Noodles 85
- **Conclusion** 87

INTRODUCTION

Vegetables are known to be high in water (vegetables such as zucchinis) and help detox your body, ridding it of unwanted toxins and can even help spike the metabolism leaving you refreshed and hydrated. Vegetables have enormous dietary fiber, which helps keep you fuller longer and help with your daily digestion

It has been proven by researcher that a healthy whole-food plant-based diet lowers cholesterol, can reverse diabetes, significantly reduces the risk of heart disease, prevents cancer and lowers blood pressure. With *The 22-Day Rev' spiralizer cookbook*, you'll have the guidance to adopt a plant-based diet and create lifelong habits that not only help you avoid serious health issues, but also shed weight faster and improve your overall life.

However, with spiralizing, a small vegetable can yield many cups of fluffy, spiral vegetables. In the same vein, you are meant to understand that vegetables and fruits go a long way, so you basically consume a lesser amount of whole vegetables, while feeling like you're eating a big portion, on account of the noodle shape of spiralized vegetables.

Finally, you should know that spiralized vegetables and fruits are helpful for those suffering from autoimmune diseases, such as Celiac's, while also valuable for those who subscribe to a vegan, vegetarian or Paleo lifestyle. Spiralized vegetables are for everyone irrespective of age, but they are especially helpful for those who have sensitivities to gluten, since they're naturally gluten-free. Spiralized vegetables are made of, well, vegetables! They're clean and unprocessed Unlike the Regular pasta, rice and noodles that are typically made from rice, wheat or flour.

HOW YOU CAN BEST MAINTAIN YOUR SPIRALIZER

Cleaning and storing of spiralizer

You should buy a round brush (such as the OXO Soap-Squirting Round Palm Brush) and designate it to your spiralizer.

The Oxo soap-squirting round palm brush scrub the hard-to-reach parts of your spiralizer (places like the teeth on the handle and the metal blades), it will prevent any nicks or cuts from the sharp blades and teeth.

Make sure you rinse and clean your spiralizer immediately after using to avoid discoloration (especially with beets!) So, take 20 seconds to rinse and scrub the spiralizer to enable it last longer.

Storing:

Remember, there's a "safety mode."

You first switch the blade using The Noodle Twister to Blade A (NOTE: This will ensure that no pointy blades are facing outwards, so that you will be protected when you remove it from the cupboard or shelf.

Make sure you store with the back stopper to prevent the handle from falling out and hitting the ground and allows for easy, compact storage.

Vegetable that can give you the best result when spiralized

Mooli
This vegetable is known to be part of the radish family and is used widely in Asian cooking. It can be used in place of rice noodles to make pad Thai, or raw in Asian salads.

Carrots
it exciting to know that the raw carrot ribbons, made with the slicing blade, add texture and crunch to a salad or slaw. Or better still you can stir-fry the carrot ribbons for a couple of minutes with garlic and coconut oil for a healthy side dish.

Sweet potato
You can use the thicker noodle blade to create sweet potato curly fries, all you have to do is toss in a little oil and bake until crisp.

Courgette
this vegetable will make you forget about spaghetti. You should use the thin noodle attachment on the spiralizer to create long twirls of pasta-like vegetable noodles. This you do by simply boiling the spiralised courgette for about 20 seconds, then top with Bolognese or stir through pesto and some prawns.

Apples
Remember, coleslaw will never be the same again, add texture with apple noodles; and make sure you toss in lemon juice as soon as the apple noodles come out of the spiralizer to prevent them from browning.

Zucchini and Cucumbers:

When using these vegetables, be certain that the noodles are separate from any sauce or dressing. By separating, all you have to do is avoid excess moisture building up and making a soggy mess. When using zucchini noodles, try adding elements that will soak up that moisture (such as leafy greens – like kale, cheese, etc.)

Pears:

Remember, fruits such as apple and pears brown quickly and lose their crispness, so I will suggest you avoid spiralizing these in advance unless you're planning on eating the meal that day or you don't mind a little browning and soft fruit noodles.

Kohlrabi, Jicama, Daikon Radishes:

When you using these raw and fitting them into a container, note that they'll snap easily when packed tightly.

Beets:

Remember, beets are messy when it is raw and less messy when cooked, so when packing in advance – keep this in mind and plan accordingly.

Butternut Squash:

Remember, butternut squashes tend to over-soften quickly when cooked – they break up easily and aren't the sturdiest (but are delicious!) try keeping this in mind, in case you had your heart set on a full pasta-like experience for lunch.

THE REV' SPIRALIZER COOKBOOK FOR A HEALTHIER YOU

Butternut Squash Rice, Sausage, Apple and Pecan Stuffing

Ingredients

2 tablespoons of extra virgin olive oil

6 celery ribs (diced)

4 teaspoons of dried thyme

1 ½ cups of roughly chopped pecans

4 tablespoons of chopped parsley

1 cup of shredded parmesan cheese (it is optional)

2 large butternut squash (peeled, Blade C)

6 garlic cloves (minced)

1 cup of diced yellow or better still white onion

6 sweet Italian sausage links (deceased)

2 Gala apple (Blade B)

Salt and pepper (to taste)

Directions:

1. Meanwhile, you heat the oven to 400 degrees.
2. After which you place the butternut squash noodles into a food processor.
3. After that, you pulse until rice-like.
4. Then you set aside.
5. At this point, you place a large, deep skillet over medium heat and add in the olive oil.
6. Immediately the oil heats, you add in the garlic, onion, celery, thyme and season with salt and pepper.
7. After which you cook for about 3-5 minutes or until the vegetables soften and then add in the sausage, breaking it up with a wooden spoon and cook for about 5 more minutes until it's no longer pink.
8. In addition, you add in the apples, butternut squash rice and parsley.
9. After that, you season with salt and pepper and stir to combine.
10. Cook for approximately 2-3 minutes or until everything is heated through.
11. This is when you remove from heat and transfer to a large casserole dish.
12. Furthermore, you fold in the pecans, stir once more and then top with the parmesan cheese (it is optional).

13. Finally, you bake for about 15-20 minutes or until butternut squash rice is no longer crunchy.

Nutritional value:

Amount per serving: 1 serving size

Calories: 231

Fat: 16g

Carbohydrate: 6g

Dietary fiber: 15g

Protein: 18g

Pumpkin Spice Sweet Potato Noodle Waffles (Gluten-Free)

Ingredients

2 teaspoons of pumpkin spice

2 tablespoons of maple syrup or better still more, to preference

2 medium sweet potatoes (peeled, Blade C)

2 medium eggs (beaten)

A Cooking spray

Directions:

1. First, you heat up the waffle iron.
2. After which you place a large skillet over medium heat and coat with cooking spray.
3. After that, you add the sweet potato noodles to the skillet.
4. Then you cook, turning frequently, for about 10 minutes or until noodles have completely softened.
5. In addition, you add the noodles into a bowl and add in the pumpkin spice.
6. This is when you mix to combine thoroughly.
7. Then you add in the full egg and toss to combine.
8. At this point, you spray the waffle iron with cooking spray and pack in the noodles.
9. Furthermore, you may have to play around with the noodles to get them to fit in all of the grooves.
10. After which you cook the waffle according to the iron's settings.
11. Finally, you serve with maple syrup.

Fall Harvest Butternut Squash Rice and Lentil Pilaf

Ingredients

Ingredients For the pilaf:

2 cups of water

2 tablespoons of extra virgin olive oil

2 teaspoons of fresh chopped rosemary

2 celery stalk

Salt and pepper (to taste)

1 cup of dried cranberries (preferably unsweetened – with no sugar added)

1 cup of dry lentils (any type works), rinsed

2 medium butternut squash (peeled, Blade C)

4 garlic cloves

1 sweet Vidalia onion

2 cups of sliced leeks

1 cup of chopped walnuts

Directions:

1. First, you place lentils and water in a medium saucepan and bring to a boil.
2. When it starts boiling, you lower to a simmer and cook uncovered for about 30-35 minutes or until cooked through.
3. After which you add more water to always slightly cover the lentils, as needed.
4. Furthermore, after lentils are cooked, you place the butternut squash noodles in a food processor and pulse until rice-like.
5. Then you set aside.
6. At this point, you dice the Vidalia onion, celery and mince the garlic cloves then you set aside.
7. This is when you place a large skillet over medium heat and add in the olive oil.
8. If it is heated, you add in the garlic and rosemary and cook for about 30 seconds or until fragrant.
9. After which you add in the celery, onion and leeks and cook for about 2-3 minutes or until onions are translucent and then add the butternut squash rice and season with salt and pepper.
10. In addition, you stir the butternut squash rice to combine and cover and cook for about 5-8 minutes, shaking the pan occasionally, or until cooked through (taste.)

11. Then if the squash is still crunchy, I suggest you cover the skillet and cook for about 2-3 more minutes.
12. Finally, when done, you add in the walnuts, lentils, cranberries and stir to combine for about 1-2 minutes to warm up the cranberries.
13. After that, you serve immediately.

Nutritional value:

Amount per serving: 1 serving size

Calories: 168

Fat: 12.9g

Carbohydrate: 10.7g

Dietary fiber: 1.3g

Protein: 4.6g

Roasted Butternut Squash Noodles with Orange-Cranberry Sauce & Honey Roasted Pecans

Ingredients

Ingredients For the glaze:

½ cup of water

2 cups of cranberries

Salt and pepper (to taste)

½ cup of maple syrup

½ cranberry juice

2 teaspoons of orange zest

½ cup of freshly squeezed orange juice

Ingredients For the rest:

Olive oil cooking spray

Honey (to drizzle)

2 butternut squash (peeled, Blade C)

Salt and pepper (to taste)

1 cup of pecans

Directions:

1. Meanwhile, you heat the oven to 400 degrees.
2. After which you place a medium saucepan over high heat.
3. After that, you place in all of the ingredients for the orange-cranberry glaze.
4. At this point, you cover and bring to a boil.
5. Then once it is boiling, I suggest you reduce the heat to low and simmer for approximately 15 minutes or until sauce thickens and liquids reduce.
6. Furthermore, when done, you turn off the heat, pour into a bowl and let thicken as it cools.
7. At this point, while the glaze is cooking, you should get ready to bake your noodles.
8. First, you place them in a baking tray coated with cooking spray.
9. After which you season generously with salt and pepper and then set aside.
10. After that, once the glaze is done and you've turned off the heat and set it aside in a bowl, you bake the noodles for about 5-7 minutes or until noodles wilt and become soft.
11. Then you remove from the oven and pour into a serving bowl.
12. Furthermore, you add in the pecans in one of the baking trays used.

13. This is when you drizzle with honey and place in the oven for about 3 minutes.
14. At this point, while the pecans are roasting, you stir your glaze and pour it on top of your noodles, carefully and once the pecans are done, place them on top of the glazed noodles.
15. Finally, before serving, you toss the noodles, glaze and pecans so that the glaze coats all of the noodles.

Notes

Make sure while you are cooking your glaze, that you prepare your butternut squash noodles to save time.

Nutritional value:

Amount per serving: 1 serving size

Calories: 168

Fat: 12.9g

Carbohydrate: 10.7g

Dietary fiber: 1.3g

Protein: 4.6g

Apple Tuna Salad Bell Pepper Sandwich

Ingredients

1 cup of chopped celery

4 large red bell peppers

2 large Granny Smith apple

4 packed cups of baby arugula

2 (5oz) can tuna in water

Ingredients For the mayonnaise:

2 tablespoons of whole grain (or preferably Dijon mustard)

Salt and pepper (to taste)

1 1/3 cup + 4 tablespoons of nonfat plain Greek Yogurt

1 teaspoon of garlic powder

2 tablespoons of lemon juice

Directions:

1. First, you combine all of the ingredients for the mayonnaise together in a small bowl and whisk until combined.
2. After which you set aside.
3. After that, you slice the apple halfway lengthwise and spiraled it, using Blade B.
4. Then you add the apple to a large bowl with the arugula, celery, tuna and mayonnaise.
5. At this point, you toss to combine thoroughly.
6. This is when you slice the top off of both the bell peppers and slice in half.
7. Furthermore, you deseed and remove any of the white inside flesh.
8. Finally, to assemble the sandwiches, I suggest you fill each bell pepper with the apple tuna salad

Nutritional value:

Amount per serving: 1 serving size

Calories: 98

Fat: 1g

Carbohydrate: 13g

Dietary fiber: 3g

Protein: 11g

Spinach and Apple Noodle Salad with Pecans and Cranberries

Ingredients

Ingredients For the salad:

6 apples (Blade C)

2/3 cups of dried cranberries

10 cups of baby spinach

1 cup pecans

Ingredients For the dressing:

2 tablespoons of ground Dijon mustard

2 tablespoons of honey

4 tablespoons of extra virgin olive oil

Salt and pepper (to taste)

4 tablespoons of balsamic vinegar

Directions:

1. First, you place the ingredients for the dressing into a bowl and whisk together until combined.
2. After which you set aside.
3. After that, you place all of the ingredients for the salad into a large serving or salad bowl and pour over the dressing.
4. Finally, you toss to combine thoroughly and serve.

Nutritional value:

Amount per serving: 1 serving size

Calories: 346

Fat: 23g

Carbohydrate: 38g

Dietary fiber: 6g

Protein: 3g

Easy Apple Noodle & Rhubarb Crisps

Ingredients

6 apples (I suggest you use gala and honey crisp), Blade C

1 cup of granola of choice (preferably Udi's Gluten Free - vanilla granola)

6 rhubarb stalks

Honey (to drizzle)

Directions:

1. Meanwhile, you heat the oven to a temperature of 350 degrees.
2. After which you take your rhubarb and slice lengthwise down the stalk. Then, cube.
3. After that, you toss the rhubarb with the apple noodles in a bowl.
4. At this point, you take out four ramekins and in each ramekin, you pack in the apple-rhubarb mixture three-quarters of the way full (I suggest you leave room at the top for the granola).
5. Furthermore, you lightly drizzle the tops of each ramekin with honey and then bake for about 30 minutes.
6. Finally, after 30 minutes, you remove the ramekins and place 4 teaspoons of granola on top per ramekin.
7. Then you bake for about 5 more minutes.
8. Once done, you are free to serve.

Nutritional value:

Amount per serving: 1 serving size

Calories: 125

Fat: 3g

Carbohydrate: 24g

Dietary fiber: 4g

Protein: 2g

Inspiralized Kale Waldorf salad

Ingredients:

Ingredients For the salad:

8 cups of chopped kale

10-14 green grapes (halved)

2 chicken breast, grilled/cooked and cut into strips

2 red apples (Blade C)

1 cup of walnuts

1 cup of celery (chopped)

For the vinaigrette (makes 1 ½ cup, only need 6 tablespoons per serving)

4 tablespoons of red wine vinegar

2 tablespoons of sherry vinegar

2 tablespoons of minced shallot

6 tablespoons of olive oil

    4 tablespoons of honey

6 tablespoons of ground Dijon mustard (or betters still less, if you don't like spicy)

2 tablespoons of water

Directions:

1. First, you place all of the ingredients for the vinaigrette into a container and shake until combined or place in a bowl and whisk.
2. After which you set aside.
3. After that, you place kale and celery in a bowl.
4. Then you pour in vinaigrette and toss to combine.
5. Finally, you divide onto plates and then top with walnuts, spiralized apple grapes, and chicken.

Nutritional value:

Amount per serving: 1 serving size

Calories: 168

Fat: 12.9g

Carbohydrate: 10.7g

Dietary fiber: 1.3g

Protein: 4.6g

Maple Brussel Sprout & Ham Hash with Apple Noodles

Ingredients

½ teaspoons of red pepper flakes

4 shallots (minced)

2 tablespoons of maple syrup

4 apples (I suggest you use a red Brae burn), Blade C

2 tablespoons of olive oil

2 small garlic clove (minced)

16-20 whole Brussel sprouts

½ cup of chicken broth

1 cup of ham in half-inch cubes

Directions:

1. First, you slice the ends off each Brussel sprout, remove the outer leaves and quarter lengthwise.
2. After which you set aside.
3. After that, you place a large skillet over medium heat and add in the olive oil.
4. Immediately the oil heats, you add in the garlic and cook for about 1 minute.
5. Then you add in the red pepper flakes and shallots and cook for about 1 minute or until the shallots soften.
6. Furthermore, you add the Brussel sprouts to the pan and cook for about 5-7 minutes, tossing frequently.
7. At this point, once Brussel sprouts have softened and lightly browned, you then drizzle with the maple syrup and add in the chicken broth and ham.
8. This is when you stir to combine thoroughly and cook for about 2 minutes or until the broth reduces and thickens.
9. Then you pour the mixture into a mixing bowl.
10. In addition, you use a scissor, cut the apple noodles so that they are no more than 6" each noodle.
11. After that, you add in the apple noodles and toss carefully to combine.
12. Finally, you plate into a serving platter and enjoy!

Nutritional value:

Amount per serving: 1 serving size

Calories: 168

Fat: 12.9g

Carbohydrate: 10.7g

Dietary fiber: 1.3g

Protein: 4.6g

Easy Apple Crisp with Peanut Butter Granola

Ingredients

2 Brae burn or preferably Honey crisp apple, Blade A

2 cups of KIND's Peanut Butter Whole Grain Clusters granola

4 Granny Smith apples, Blade A

½ cup of maple syrup

2 teaspoons of ground cinnamon

Directions:

1. Meanwhile, you heat the oven to a temperature of 400 degrees.
2. After which you place the apple slices in a bowl, drizzle with half of the maple syrup.
3. After that, you mix to combine and lay into the bottom of a small cast-iron skillet.
4. Then you bake in the oven for about 5 minutes and then remove, sprinkle over the granola to cover the apples and drizzle with remaining maple syrup.
5. Finally, you bake the crisp for about 10-15 minutes or until the apples soften completely.
6. This is when you remove from the oven and enjoy!

Nutritional value:

Amount per serving: 1 serving size

Calories: 168

Fat: 12.9g

Carbohydrate: 10.7g

Dietary fiber: 1.3g

Protein: 4.6g

Beet Noodles with Tomatoes, Feta and Bacon

Ingredients

2 large (or preferably 4 medium) red beets, peeled, Blade C/D

2 large garlic clove (finely minced)

4-6 tablespoons of crumbled feta cheese

6-8 strips of bacon of choice

1 cup of cherry tomatoes

Salt and pepper (to taste)

2 tablespoons of chopped parsley (to garnish)

Directions:

1. First, you place a large skillet over medium-high heat and coat with cooking spray and once it is heated, you add in the bacon strips and cook for about 7 minutes until crisp.
2. After which you transfer to a paper towel lined plate.
3. After that, you remove about half of the bacon fat from the skillet and set the skillet aside for about 1-2 minutes to cool down and then place back over heat.
4. Then you add in the beet noodles and toss for about 1 minute or until the noodles begin to wilt.
5. At this point, you add in the tomatoes, salt, garlic, pepper.
6. Furthermore, you cover and let cook for about 5-7 minutes, uncovering occasionally to toss, or until beet noodles are wilted and cooked to al dente.
7. Finally, once it is done, transfer the beet noodle mixture to a serving platter, crumble over with the bacon and garnish with parsley and feta.
8. Then you serve immediately.

Nutritional value:

Amount per serving: 1 serving size

Calories: 138

Fat: 8g

Carbohydrate: 10g

Dietary fiber: 2g

Protein: 8g

Jalapeno-Citrus Golden Beet Noodle Salad with Crab, Avocado and Toasted Almonds

Ingredients

Ingredients For the salad:

8 large golden beets (peeled, Blade C)

2 avocado, peeled, pitted and insides sliced thinly

½ cup of slivered almonds

4-6 cups of watercress greens

2 cups of lump crab meat

Ingredients For the dressing:

4 tablespoons of extra virgin olive oil

1 tablespoon of fresh lemon juice

¼ teaspoon of lemon zest

Salt and pepper (to taste)

1 ½ tablespoons of finely chopped shallot

3 tablespoons of apple cider vinegar

1 tablespoon of fresh orange juice

1 ½ teaspoons of seeded and finely diced jalapeno

2 teaspoons of honey

Directions:

1. First, you place a medium skillet over medium-high heat.
2. Then once it is heated, you add in the almonds and then toast, stirring occasionally, for about 2 minutes until golden brown and fragrant.
3. In the meantime, you whisk together all of the ingredients for the dressing.
4. After which you taste and adjust to your preferences.
5. After that, you toss together the beets, watercress, crab and dressing in a large bowl.
6. At this point, you divide into plates.
7. Finally, you garnish with avocado and toasted almonds.

Nutritional value:

Amount per serving: 1 serving size

Calories: 278

Fat: 19g

Carbohydrate: 16g

Dietary fiber: 7g

Protein: 14g

Beet Noodle, Pea and Arugula Salad with Lemon-Garlic Tahini Sauce

Ingredients

Ingredients For the dressing:

4 tablespoons of freshly squeezed lemon juice

2 garlic clove (minced)

Salt & pepper (to taste)

4 tablespoons of tahini

4 teaspoons of honey

2 tablespoons of extra virgin olive oil

2-4 tablespoons of water

Ingredients For the rest:

2 cups of arugula

3 cups of cooked peas

2 large beet (or preferably 4 medium), peeled, Blade C

Directions:

1. Meanwhile, you heat the oven to a temperature of 425 degrees.
2. After which you whisk together all of the ingredients (except for the water) in a medium bowl or pulse in a food processor until creamy.
3. After that, you add water as needed to make it creamy.
4. At this point, you taste and adjust to your preference.
5. Furthermore, you line a baking sheet with parchment paper and lay out the beet noodles.
6. After that, you drizzle with the olive oil and toss together to coat.
7. This is when you season with salt and pepper and roast for about 10 minutes or until softened.
8. In addition, you toss together the beets and peas in a bowl.
9. After which you transfer to a serving bowl or plate and drizzle with lemon-tahini sauce.
10. Finally, you serve a top a bed of greens (it is optional).
11. Then serve with extra sauce.

Nutritional value:

Amount per serving: 1 serving size

Calories: 291

Fat: 16g

Carbohydrate: 28g

Dietary fiber: 7g

Protein: 9g

Raw Beet Noodle and Rainbow Chard Salad with Avocado-Ranch Dressing

Ingredients

Ingredients For the salad:

12 packets of Nourish Snacks Ménage-a-Mix (or 3 cups mix of chickpeas, edamame and corn)

6 large beets, peeled, Blade C, noodles trimmed

10-12 cups of chopped Rainbow Swiss Chard

Ingredients For the dressing:

2 cups of plain almond milk (or preferably full-fat coconut milk)

4 teaspoons of red wine vinegar

3 teaspoons of freshly minced dill

1 teaspoon of onion powder

Pepper to taste

2 ripe avocadoes

6 tablespoons of freshly squeezed lemon juice

4 garlic cloves (minced)

4 teaspoons of freshly minced parsley

2 teaspoons of paprika

Salt to taste (about ½ teaspoon)

Directions:

1. First, you combine all of the ingredients for the dressing into a high speed blender or food processor and pulse until creamy.
2. After which you taste and adjust to your preferences and then set aside.
3. After that, you toss the chard and beet noodles together in a large mixing bowl.
4. Then you drizzle over with avocado-ranch dressing and let sit for about 10 minutes to soften the beet and chard.
5. At this point, when ready to serve, you divide into plates and top each with 1 packet of Nourish Snacks' Ménage-a-Mix.
6. However, if you serving family-style, I suggest you add the packets to a serving bowl with the beet and chard and toss together to combine.

Nutritional value:

Amount per serving: 6.0 serving size

Calories: 246

Fat: 10g

Carbohydrate: 31g

Dietary fiber: 9g

Protein: 9g

Crunchy Miso Beet Rice with Spinach and Egg

Ingredients

Ingredients For the miso dressing:

4 tablespoons of rice vinegar

2 tablespoons of sesame oil

2 tablespoons of water

2 tablespoons of miso

1 teaspoon of grated fresh ginger

1 tablespoon of honey

Ingredients For the rice:

4 cups of spinach

4 eggs

2 large beet, peeled, Blade C

4 scallions (diced)

1 teaspoon of sesame seeds (to garnish)

Directions:

1. First, you combine all of the ingredients for the miso dressing into a small bowl and whisk until fully combined then you set aside.
2. After which you place the beet noodles into a food processor and pulse until rice-like.
3. After that, you set aside in a medium mixing bowl.
4. This is when you place a large skillet over medium heat and add in the spinach.
5. Then you cook for about 5 minutes or until spinach wilts.
6. Furthermore, you add the spinach and miso dressing to the bowl with the beet rice, and toss to combine.
7. After that, you divide the rice into two bowls and set aside.
8. At this point, you crack in the eggs in the same skillet.
9. Make sure you let eggs cook until whites set and then top each bowl of rice with an egg and garnish with scallions and sesame seeds.

Nutritional value:

Amount per serving: 2.0 serving size

Calories: 138

Fat: 8g

Carbohydrate: 16g

Dietary fiber: 4g

Protein: 4g

Thyme Beet Risotto with Walnuts

Ingredients

2 tablespoons of extra-virgin olive oil

4 tablespoons of minced shallots

2 teaspoons of fresh thyme leaves

½ cup of grated parmesan cheese

4 large beets (peeled, Blade C)

2 clove of garlic (minced)

Salt and pepper (to taste)

½ cup of vegetable broth

2/3 cup of roughly chopped walnuts

Directions:

1. First, you place the beet noodles into a food processor and pulse until rice-like (NOTE: Be careful not to over-pulse, so go slowly).
2. After which you heat the olive oil in a large skillet over medium-heat.
3. At this point, when it is heated, you add in the garlic and shallots.
4. After that, you let cook for about 30 seconds or until fragrant and then add in the beets.
5. This is when you season the beets with pepper, salt and add in the thyme.
6. Furthermore, you stir to combine and add in the vegetable broth.
7. Then you bring to a boil and then lower to a simmer.
8. In addition, you let cook for about 5-7 minutes or until beets soften and once it softened, you remove from heat, stir in the parmesan cheese and walnuts.
9. After which you stir until cheese melts into the risotto.
10. Then you serve immediately.

Nutritional value:

Amount per serving: 3.0 serving

Calories: 263

Fat: 25g

Carbohydrate: 10g

Dietary fiber: 3g

Protein: 3g

Beet Noodle, Feta and Avocado Omelet

Ingredients

1 tablespoon of extra virgin olive oil

2 small beet, peeled, Blade C, noodles trimmed (better still only use about 1/2 cup of noodles - save the rest for future use)

6 eggs (beaten)

Salt and pepper (to taste)

6 tablespoons of crumbled feta cheese

½ of the insides of an avocado (cubed)

Freshly minced parsley (to garnish)

Directions:

1. First, you place a large skillet over medium heat and add in the olive oil.
2. When the oil heats, you add in the beet noodles.
3. After which you toss to coat in the oil and cover.
4. Cook for about 5-7 minutes or until beet noodles soften completely, uncovering occasionally to toss.

Directions For a scramble:

1. First, you add the eggs and avocado into the pan with the beet noodles and scramble together.
2. When the eggs are almost completely scrambled, you add in the feta and finish scrambling.
3. Then you serve.

Direction For an omelet:

1. First, you set the beet noodles aside.
2. After which you place a medium saucepan over medium heat (or preferably your omelet pan) and coat with cooking spray.
3. After that, you add in the eggs and let set, pulling in the edges of the eggs with a spatula to let the egg disperse and cook almost fully.
4. Then once most of the eggs are set, you season with salt and pepper and add in the beet noodles, feta and avocado.
5. Furthermore, you fold the omelet in half and press down to compress with the back of a spatula.
6. At this point, you let cook for another 2 minutes or until eggs are cooked through.
7. Finally, you garnish with parsley and serve.

Nutritional value:

Amount per serving: 5.0 serving

Calories: 159

Fat: 11g

Carbohydrate: 15g

Dietary fiber: 4g

Protein: 3g

Roasted Beet Noodles with Pesto and Baby Kale

Ingredients

4 cups of baby kale

4 medium beets (peeled, Blade C, noodles trimmed)

Olive oil cooking spray

Ingredients For the pesto:

½ cup of peanuts

1 teaspoon of grinded sea salt

2 large clove of garlic (minced)

6 cups of basil leaves (packed)

½ cup of olive oil

½ teaspoon of grinded pepper

Directions:

1. Preheat the oven to a temperature of 425 degrees.
2. After which you spread out the beet noodles on a baking sheet, and coat with cooking spray and season with salt and pepper.
3. Then you bake for about 5-10 minutes or until beets are cooked to al dente or your preference in doneness.
4. At this point, while the noodles cook, you combine all of the ingredients for the pesto into a food processor and pulse until creamy.
5. After that, you taste and adjust, if needed.
6. Finally, once the beets are cooked, you toss with pesto and the kale.
7. Then you serve.

Nutritional value:

Amount per serving: 1 serving size

Calories: 168

Fat: 12.9g

Carbohydrate: 10.7g

Dietary fiber: 1.3g

Protein: 4.6g

Mini Cheese Plate with Warm Beet Noodles

Ingredients

1 tablespoon of extra virgin olive oil

2 (5oz) roll of goat cheese

4 tablespoons of honey

2 medium beet (peeled, Blade C, noodles trimmed)

Salt and pepper (to taste)

½ cup of whole pecans

Directions:

1. Meanwhile, you heat the oven to a temperature of 425 degrees.
2. After which you place the beet noodles out on a baking sheet and drizzle with the olive oil.
3. After that, you toss to combine and season with salt and pepper.
4. Then you bake for about 7-10 minutes or until softened.
5. This is when you remove from the oven and place in a medium bowl (preferably a 6oz ramekin).
6. At this point, you assemble your cheese plate and place the bowl of beets on one end of the cheese plate, with serving utensils.
7. Furthermore, you place on the goat cheese with a spreading knife.
8. After which, you lightly crush the pecans using the back of a knife or spatula.
9. Then you place them in a small bowl on the cheese board.
10. In addition, you place the honey in a small bowl with a serving spoon and onto the cheese board/plate.
11. Finally, you serve and impress your guests!

Nutritional value:

Amount per serving: 3.0 serving

Calories: 236

Fat: 17g

Carbohydrate: 16g

Dietary fiber: 2g

Protein: 8g

Quick Pickled Beets and Yellow Wax Beans with Feta and Chives

Ingredients

2 (7.5oz) yellow wax beans (ends trimmed)

½ cup of apple cider vinegar

2/3 cup of minced chives

4 medium beets (peeled, Blade C, noodles trimmed)

½ teaspoon of coarse salt (to taste)

4 tablespoon of extra virgin olive oil

½ cup of crumbled feta cheese

Directions:

1. First, you bring a medium pot filled halfway with water to a boil and once boiling, add in the beets and wax beans.
2. After that, while water is waiting to boil, you fill a medium bowl with ice and set aside.
3. This is when you let the beets and wax beans cook for about 5 minutes or until beans are easily pierced with a fork and then drain into a colander and place over ice.
4. Then you toss the veggies in the ice and once cooled, place in a bowl with the salt, pepper, apple cider vinegar and olive oil.
5. Furthermore, you set aside in the refrigerator for about 20 minutes at the least, but the longer the better.
6. After which you remove the bowl from the fridge.
7. At this point, you place a colander over a bowl and drain the noodles into the colander, reserving the juice.
8. After that, you place the noodles into a bowl, add in half of the reserved juices and then add in the chives and feta to the bowl.
9. Finally, you toss to combine and serve.

Nutritional value:

Amount per serving: 3.0 serving

Calories: 138

Fat: 9g

Carbohydrate: 10g

Dietary fiber: 4g

Protein: 4g

Candy Cane Beet Noodle and Arugula Quinoa Salad with Parmesan-Garlic Vinaigrette

Ingredients

2 large Chioggia Guardsmark beet (peeled, Blade C)

4 tablespoons of grated parmesan cheese

½ cup of quinoa

1 cup of water

4 cups of baby arugula

2/3 cup of quartered pitted green olives

<u>Ingredients For the vinaigrette:</u>

4 tablespoons of red wine vinegar

6 tablespoons of extra virgin olive oil

2 clove of garlic

Salt and pepper (to taste)

Directions:

1. First, you place the quinoa and water in a small saucepan and bring to a boil.
2. Immediately it starts boiling, reduce to a simmer and cook for about 15 minutes or until quinoa is fluffy.
3. After which you add more water if needed.
4. After that, while quinoa is cooking, you prepare the vinaigrette.
5. Then you add the garlic to a mortar (if you don't have a mortar, I suggest you crush in a bowl) and lightly season with salt.
6. At this point, you grind into a puree and pour in the vinegar.
7. Furthermore, you season with pepper and mix.
8. This is when you pour mixture into a bowl or dressing shaker and add in the olive oil.
9. After that, you mix to combine.
10. Then you combine the beets, olives and arugula in a large mixing bowl.
11. In addition, you pour over the dressing, add in the cheese and toss to thoroughly combine.
12. After which you let sit while the quinoa still cooks.
13. Finally, when quinoa is done, you add it to the mixing bowl and toss to combine.
14. Then you serve.

Nutritional value:

Amount per serving: 3.0 serving

Calories: 191

Fat: 24g

Carbohydrate: 14g

Dietary fiber: 2g

Protein: 6g

Chilled Sweet and Sour Cucumber Noodles

Ingredients:

1 cup of diced red onion

5 teaspoons of sugar

3 teaspoons of white sesame seeds

4 medium cucumbers {peeled}

1 ½ cup of rice vinegar

1 teaspoon of crushed red pepper flakes (it is optional)

Equipment: a mandolin or spiralizer

Directions:

1. First, you attach the julienne blade to the mandolin or spiralizer.
2. After which you adjust it to the 1/8-inch-thick setting.
3. In addition, applying medium pressure, you carefully run one of the cucumbers down the blade to form noodles, slicing until you reach the core.
4. After that, you rotate the cucumber a quarter turn and continue slicing and rotating until you've cut the entire cucumber.
5. This is when you repeat the slicing process with the second cucumber then transfer the cucumber noodles to a medium bowl.
6. Then you add the red onion, ½ cup water, rice vinegar, sugar and crushed red pepper flakes (it is optional) to the bowl.
7. Furthermore, you cover the bowl with plastic wrap and refrigerate the cucumber noodles for a minimum of 2 hours, stirring occasionally, until chilled.
8. Finally, when it ready to serve, use tongs or a slotted spoon to transfer the noodles to serving plates.
9. After which you top with the sesame seeds.

Dan Noodles & Pickled Cucumber Salad

Yield: 8 servings

Ingredients:

INGREDIENTS For the pickled cucumber salad:

1 cup of red onion (thinly sliced)

4 cups of cucumbers (thinly sliced)

1 ½ cups of rice wine (or preferably white wine vinegar)

2 Tablespoons of sugar

2 teaspoons of salt

INGREDIENTS For the noodles:

½ cup of dry sherry

6 heaping Tablespoons of chunky peanut butter

2 Tablespoons of brown sugar

2 teaspoons of toasted sesame oil

4 Tablespoons of finely grated fresh ginger

24 ounces of ground turkey

1 pound pasta (preferably Whole Wheat Linguine)

½ cup of chicken broth

4 Tablespoons of soy sauce

2 Tablespoons of chili garlic sauce

½ cup of red bell pepper (small dice)

4 Tablespoons of minced garlic

Directions:

Directions For the pickled cucumbers:

1. First, you combine all ingredients.
2. After which you taste and adjust seasoning.
3. Finally, you refrigerate until ready to serve.

Directions For the noodles:

1. First, you cook the pasta in salted boiling water until al dente.
2. After which you strain and reserve.
3. After that, you whisk together the dry sherry, peanut butter, chicken broth, brown sugar, chili garlic sauce, soy sauce, and toasted sesame oil.
4. Then you reserve, after that you sauté the garlic, ginger and red pepper in a small amount of oil for 2-3 minutes. Then you reserve.
5. This is when you brown the ground turkey in a large sauté pan until cooked fully.
6. Furthermore, you add the sautéed aromatics to the turkey.
7. After that, you pour the reserved peanut sauce into the pan with the browned turkey and cook on medium heat just until sauce thickens.
8. Then you add the noodles to the pan and toss to coat.
9. Finally, you serve the noodles with the Pickled Cucumber Salad.

Spicy Moroccan Chickpeas with Beet Noodles

Ingredients

4 tablespoons of extra virgin olive oil

1 red onion (finely chopped)

2 teaspoons of gram masala

Salt and pepper (to taste)

2 tablespoons of lemon juice

2 (14oz) diced tomatoes (no salt added)

6-8 large beets, peeled, Blade C, noodles trimmed

4 teaspoons of minced garlic

14 dried apricots (small cubed)

2 teaspoons of cumin

½ teaspoons of crushed red pepper

2 (14oz) can chickpeas, drained, rinsed, patted dry

2 tablespoons of chopped fresh mint

Directions

1. Meanwhile, you heat the oven to a temperature of 400 degrees.
2. After which you lay out the beet noodles evenly in a baking tray and drizzle with 2 tablespoons of the olive oil.
3. After that, you season with salt and pepper and bake for about 10-15 minutes or until wilted.
4. Then you heat a large skillet over medium-high heat.
5. At this point, you add in the rest of the olive oil and once it heats, add in garlic.
6. Furthermore, you cook the garlic for 30 seconds or until fragrant.
7. After which you add the apricots, lemon juice, garam masala, onions, red pepper flakes and season with salt and pepper.
8. Then you cook for about 5 minutes or until onion begins to slightly brown.
9. In addition, you add in the chickpeas and tomatoes and bring to a boil.
10. After that, you reduce the heat and simmer for about 5-7 minutes, stirring occasionally, to reduce.
11. When it is reduced, stir in the mint.
12. Finally, you divide the beet noodles onto 8 plates and top each with hearty scoops of the chickpea mixture

Nutritional value:

Amount per serving: 4.0 serving

Calories: 319

Fat: 10g

Carbohydrate: 49g

Dietary fiber: 12g

Protein: 12g

Sparkling Cider Glazed Roasted Beet Noodles with Crispy Shallots

Ingredients

Ingredients For the cider glaze:

4 cups of sparkling apple cider (I prefer Martin Elli's)

Salt and pepper (to taste)

½ cup of apple cider vinegar

4 tablespoons of maple syrup

2 teaspoons of regular Dijon mustard

Ingredients For the rest:

Olive oil to drizzle

½ cup of olive oil

4 large beets (peeled, Blade C)

24 large shallots (sliced thinly)

Directions:

1. Meanwhile, you heat the oven to a temperature of 400 degrees.
2. After which you place a large skillet over high heat and add in the olive oil.
3. After that, you cook the oil until it starts to smoke and lower the heat to medium.
4. Then you add in the sliced shallots and cook, stirring frequently, for 3 minutes or until shallots brown.
5. As soon as it is done, you transfer with a slotted spoon to a paper towel lined plate and then set aside.
6. This is when you add all of the ingredients for the glaze into a medium size saucepan and bring to a boil.
7. As soon as it starts boiling, you lower to a medium simmer and cook for about 10-15 minutes or until it reduces and becomes a glaze.
8. As soon as it starts foaming, you stir the glaze nonstop until it reaches a thick consistency.
9. Remember it's alright if it's liquidly, it will thicken as it cools.
10. At this point, while the glaze is cooking, you add the beet noodles into a baking tray, drizzle with olive oil and season with salt and pepper.
11. Then you roast for about 5-8 minutes or until noodles wilt.
12. Finally, when beet noodles are done, you place them in a serving platter, drizzle with the cider glaze and top with crispy shallots.
13. Enjoy!

Nutritional value:

Amount per serving: 1 serving size

Calories: 168

Fat: 12.9g

Carbohydrate: 10.7g

Dietary fiber: 1.3g

Protein: 4.6g

Pesto Turkey & Beet Rice Lettuce Wraps

Ingredients

Ingredients For the pesto:

½ cup of pine nuts

½ cup of grated parmesan cheese

2/3 cup of olive oil

8 cups of packed basil

4 teaspoons of minced garlic

Salt and pepper (to taste)

Ingredients For the rest:

4 tablespoons olive oil

Pinches of red pepper flakes

1-2/3 pound lean ground turkey

4 heads of Bibb lettuce

2 very large beet (peeled, Blade C)

4 garlic cloves (minced)

1 cup of diced red onion

½ cup of chicken broth

2 teaspoons of dried oregano flakes

Directions:

1. First, you take your spiralized beet noodles and place them into a food processor.
2. After which you pulse until made into rice-like bits then you set aside.
3. After that, you place all of your ingredients for the pesto into a food processor and pulse until creamy.
4. Then you taste and adjust to your preference.
5. Furthermore, you place a large skillet over medium heat and add in your olive oil.
6. As soon as oil heats, you add in your garlic and red pepper flakes.
7. At this point, you cook for about 30 seconds and then add in your red onion.
8. After which you cook the onion for about 2-3 minutes or until translucent and then add in your turkey meat, oregano and season with salt and pepper.
9. This is when you cook the turkey meat for about 5 minutes until no longer pink.

10. In addition, you add in the chicken broth and let reduce and once reduced, add in the beet rice and toss to combine.
11. After that, you let the beet rice cook, stirring frequently, for about 5 minutes.
12. Remember if watery (from the beet juice), I suggest you pour the contents of the skillet into a colander, drain and put back into the skillet.
13. After which you fold in the pesto sauce.
14. Finally, you stir to combine and cook for 1 minute.
15. Then when it is done, you spoon into lettuce wraps and enjoy!

Nutritional value:

Amount per serving: 1 serving size

Calories: 168

Fat: 12.9g

Carbohydrate: 10.7g

Dietary fiber: 1.3g

Protein: 4.6g

Roasted Orange & Beet Noodle Pasta with Honey Walnuts & Crispy Baked Kale

Ingredients

Ingredients For the vinaigrette:

2 crank of the salt grinder

2 tablespoons of olive oil

1 teaspoon of country Dijon mustard

Juice from ½ of a large lemon

4 cranks of a pepper grinder

2 teaspoons of red wine vinegar

3 tablespoons of orange juice

Ingredients For the rest:

2 large orange (peeled and sliced into fourths or eighths)

Olive oil (to drizzle)

A handful of walnuts

Raw honey (to drizzle)

Olive oil cooking spray

2 cups of roughly chopped kale leaves (preferably with stems removed)

2 large beet (peeled, Blade C)

Directions:

1. Meanwhile, you heat the oven to a temperature of 375 degrees.
2. After which in a baking tray lightly coated with cooking spray, you place in the orange slices on one side and the kale on the other.
3. After that, you lightly coat the kale with the cooking spray and season with pepper.
4. Then you set the timer for about 20 minutes.
5. After approximately 10-12 minutes, you remove the kale from the baking tray and set aside.
6. Furthermore, you place the baking tray with the oranges back into the oven.
7. Place the beet noodles in another baking tray and drizzle lightly with olive oil.
8. Then you season with salt and pepper and roast in the oven for approximately 10-15 minutes.
9. At this point, while the oranges and beets are roasting, you assemble your vinaigrette.

10. After that, you place all ingredients into a bowl, whisk together and place in the refrigerator.
11. In about 5 minutes before the oranges are done, you place the walnuts on the side of the baking tray that used to hold the kale.
12. In addition, you drizzle lightly with honey and toss carefully with tongs.
13. After which you let roast for the remaining 5 minutes and take out with the oranges.
14. Then when the beet noodles are done (it should be done with the oranges or have another 5 minutes left).
15. Finally, you place them in a bowl and top with the orange slices, walnuts and kale.
16. This is when you drizzle the vinaigrette over and enjoy!

Nutritional value:

Amount per serving: 1 serving size

Calories: 168

Fat: 12.9g

Carbohydrate: 10.7g

Dietary fiber: 1.3g

Protein: 4.6g

Garlic Broccoli Noodles with Toasted Pine Nuts

Ingredients

4 tablespoons of olive oil

Salt and pepper (to taste)

4 garlic cloves (thinly sliced)

2 tablespoons of grated pecorino Romano cheese

2 large broccoli head with stem

2 pinches of red pepper flakes

2 tablespoons of pine nuts

2 tablespoons of fresh lemon juice

Directions:

1. First, you slice off the head of the broccoli, leaving as little stem on the florets as possible.
2. After which you set aside the broccoli florets and then slice the bottom end of the broccoli stem so that it is evenly flat.
3. After that, you spiraled the broccoli stem, using Blade C.
4. At this point, you place a large skillet over medium heat and add in the olive oil.
5. As soon as the oil heats, you add in the broccoli florets, red pepper flakes, stems and season with salt and pepper.
6. Then you cover and cook for about 3-5 minutes, shaking the skillet frequently, letting the broccoli cook.
7. Furthermore, while the broccoli is cooking, place your pine nuts in a small skillet over medium heat.
8. After which you let toast for about 5 minutes until fragrant and the pine nuts slightly brown (carefully, not to burn the pine nuts – toss occasionally.
9. Then when done, you set aside.
10. In addition, you add in the garlic and lemon juice and cook for about 3-5 more minutes (covered) or until broccoli is tender but more easily pierced with a fork.
11. After that, you transfer the broccoli to a serving bowl and top with pine nuts and pecorino Romano cheese.

Nutritional value:

Amount per serving: 2.0 serving

Calories: 214

Fat: 15g

Carbohydrate: 18g

Dietary fiber: 6g

Protein: 8g

Spicy Tilapia and Black Radish Spaghetti with Cilantro-Jalapeno Avocado Tomato Sauce

Ingredients

1 cup of diced white onions

2 garlic clove (minced)

Salt and pepper (to taste)

1 avocado, peeled, insides cubed into ¼" pieces

2 (6oz) tilapia, cut into 1" chunks

2 tablespoons of extra virgin olive oil

1 jalapeno (seeded, finely diced)

2 (29 oz.) can whole peeled tomatoes

2 large black radish, Blade C, noodles trimmed

2 tablespoons of chopped cilantro

Directions:

1. First you place a large skillet over medium heat and add in half of the oil.
2. As soon as the oil heats, you add in the jalapenos onions, and garlic.
3. After which you let cook for about 2-3 minutes or until onions are translucent.
4. After that, you add in the tomatoes and juices, crushing with your hands over the skillet.
5. At this point, you season with salt and pepper and let cook for about 5-7 minutes or until sauce thickens.
6. As soon as the sauce is almost done, you add another large skillet over medium heat and add in the rest of the olive oil.
7. Then once it's heated, you add in the radish noodles and season with salt and pepper.
8. Furthermore, you cover and cook, uncovering occasionally to toss, for about 5-7 minutes or until cooked to al dente.
9. After that you add the radish noodles to the skillet, stir in the avocado and cilantro into the tomato sauce and then add in the tilapia, nestling it into the sauce.
10. Then you let cook, covered, for about 3-5 minutes or until opaque and cooked through.
11. Finally, you divide the radish noodles into bowls and top with tomato sauce.
12. Make sure you serve immediately.

Nutritional value:

Amount per serving: 1 serving size

Calories: 168

Fat: 12.9g

Carbohydrate: 10.7g

Dietary fiber: 1.3g

Protein: 4.6g

Spiral zed Garlic-Paprika Sweet Potato "Fries"

Ingredients

2 tablespoons of extra virgin olive oil

2 teaspoons of paprika

2 sweet potato (peeled, Blade D)

Salt, to taste (remember, make sure you're using a sea salt grinder - makes such a difference)

2 teaspoons of garlic powder

Note: If you don't have the Inspiralizer, feel free to use the smallest noodle blade on your version

Directions:

1. Meanwhile, you heat the oven to a temperature of 400 degrees.
2. After which you spread the noodles out on a large baking tray and drizzle with the olive oil.
3. After that, you toss the noodles together gently with your fingers, coating the noodles in the oil.
4. Then you season with paprika, salt and garlic powder.
5. At this point, you roast for about 20 minutes, tossing halfway through (gently and be careful not to break the tender noodles)
6. Furthermore, after about 15 minutes, you make sure to check the noodles to prevent burning (note: If it starts to burn, toss those pieces gently.
7. Finally, you serve, discarding any completely burnt pieces, with favorite dip or ketchup.

Nutritional value:

Amount per serving: 1 serving size

Calories: 168

Fat: 12.9g

Carbohydrate: 10.7g

Dietary fiber: 1.3g

Protein: 4.6g

Roasted Sweet Potato and Yam Noodles with Fennel, Charred Tomatoes, Olives and Pecorino

Ingredients

2 medium sweet potato (peeled, Blade C)

8 tablespoons of extra-virgin olive oil

½ cup of freshly grated pecorino cheese

8 plum tomatoes, thudded

4 tablespoons of chopped fresh flat-leaf parsley

4 large bulbs fennel (quartered)

2 medium yam (peeled, Blade C)

Kosher salt and freshly ground pepper (to taste)

1 teaspoon of oregano

2/3 cup of pitted Kalamata olives (halved)

NOTE: To prepare, you slice the very ends off and then cut the stalks off the bulb so that little to no stalk remains on the bulb. Then you quarter.

Directions:

1. Meanwhile, you heat the oven to a temperature of 375 degrees F.
2. After which you toss together half of the olive oil and the potato noodles in a large bowl.
3. After that, you arrange the potato noodles into a skillet or baking dish so that it fits in one layer and season with salt and pepper.
4. Then you add in the rest of the olive oil with the fennel in the same bowl.
5. At this point, you toss lightly and arrange the seasoned fennel on top of the sweet potato noodles in an even layer.
6. Furthermore, you dust with the oregano and season with salt and pepper.
7. After which you add half of the pecorino cheese on top, sprinkling all over to coat the fennel and sweet potatoes.
8. This is when you roast for about 50 minutes until the fennel is fork tender.
9. Then you remove the dish from the oven and turn to broil.
10. After that, you lay the tomatoes on top of the fennel and sweet potatoes, cut-side up.
11. At this point, you return the dish to the oven and broil the tomatoes for about 6 to 8 minutes until slightly charred and warmed through.
12. Finally, you remove the dish from the oven and immediately sprinkle over with the remaining pecorino cheese and the olives.

13. Then you garnish with the parsley and serve immediately.

Nutritional value:

Amount per serving: 1 serving size

Calories: 168

Fat: 12.9g

Carbohydrate: 10.7g

Dietary fiber: 1.3g

Protein: 4.6g

Garlic Asia go Baked Spiralized Fries

Ingredients

2 medium Idaho potato (Blade B)

2 tablespoons of garlic powder

Fine sea salt and ground pepper

2 medium sweet potato (Blade B)

4 tablespoons of extra virgin olive oil

2/3 cup of grated Asia go cheese

Directions:

1. First, you heat the oven to a temperature of 450 degrees.
2. After which you trim the potato noodles so that they are serving friendly.
3. After that, you place the potato noodles in a mixing bowl and drizzle over the olive oil, toss in the garlic powder, Asia go cheese and season generously with salt and pepper.
4. Then you toss to coat thoroughly.
5. At this point, you spread the potatoes out on a baking tray lined with nonstick parchment paper, trying not to overlap the potatoes.
6. Feel free to use two baking trays, if needed.
7. This is when you drizzle over the Asia go cheese, careful to cover all potatoes.
8. Furthermore, you bake in the oven for about 10-15 minutes and then flip over.
9. After that, you bake for another 10-15 minutes or until browned, flipping every 5 minutes if necessary (i.e. if your oven starts burning the fries.)
10. Finally, you remove from the oven and serve atop a salad, over steak, as a side or simply enjoy as a snack.

Nutritional value:

Amount per serving: 4.0 serving

Calories: 159

Fat: 10g

Carbohydrate: 15g

Dietary fiber: 2g

Protein: 4g

Spiralized Tzimmes for Rosh Hashanah

Ingredients

4 large sweet potatoes (peeled, Blade C)

Salt (to taste)

6 large carrots (peeled and cubed)

1 cup of bite-sized dried pitted prunes (roughly chopped)

1 cup of dried apricots (roughly chopped)

Ingredients For the sauce:

2 teaspoons of ground cinnamon

Zest from 2 oranges

4 tablespoons of honey

2/3 cup of fresh orange juice

4 tablespoons of fresh lemon juice

Directions:

1. Meanwhile, you heat the oven to a temperature of 350 degrees.
2. After which you bring a medium pot filled halfway with water to a boil.
3. As soon as it starts boiling, you add in the carrots and cook for about 3 minutes or until more easily pierced with a fork, but still firm.
4. After that, you drain, pat dry and set aside.
5. At this point, while the carrots are cooking, you place a large skillet over medium heat and add in the olive oil.
6. As soon as oil is heated, you toss in the sweet potato noodles and season with salt and pepper.
7. Then you cover and cook for approximately 5-7 minutes or until almost fully cooked.
8. Furthermore, you whisk together the ingredients for the sauce.
9. After which you add in the sweet potato noodles, prunes, carrots, apricots and pour over sauce in a large bowl.
10. This is when you toss to combine thoroughly and place in an 11 x 7 baking dish.
11. After that, you season lightly with salt.
12. Finally, you cover with foil, bake for about 20 minutes, basting with pan juices after 15 minutes.
13. Then you remove the dish from the oven and serve immediately.

Nutritional value:

Amount per serving: 4.0 serving

Calories: 276

Fat: 0g

Carbohydrate: 70g

Dietary fiber: 11g

Protein: 4g

Savoy Cabbage "Breakfast Burrito" with Sweet Potato Noodles

Ingredients

2 avocado (insides cubed)

pieces of bacon

6 eggs, beaten

4 cabbage savoy leafs

Salt and pepper (to taste)

2 sweet potato (peeled, Blade C)

Directions:

1. First, you rinse your cabbage leaves and pat dry then set aside, on a plate.
2. After which you place your avocado into a bowl, mash and season with salt and pepper.
3. After that, you spread this over the center of each cabbage leaf.
4. Then you place a large skillet over medium heat and add in the bacon.
5. Furthermore, you let cook until to your crispy preference and set aside on a paper-towel lined plate.
6. At this point, you remove half of the oil left behind from the bacon and add in your sweet potato noodles.
7. Then you cook the noodles, tossing occasionally, for about 5-8 minutes or until they wilt.
8. As soon as it is done, you place onto the cabbage leaves, over the avocado.
9. After that, you place the eggs into the same skillet and scramble.
10. As soon as you scrambled, you place over the sweet potato noodles.
11. Finally, you top the eggs with two pieces of bacon per wrap. Then, roll like a burrito and enjoy.

Nutritional value:

Amount per serving: 1 serving size

Calories: 168

Fat: 12.9g

Carbohydrate: 10.7g

Dietary fiber: 1.3g

Protein: 4.6g

Pesto Broccoli Sweet Potato Rice Casserole

Ingredients

Ingredients For the pesto:

4 tablespoons of pine nuts

10 cranks of the sea salt grinder

2 large clove of garlic minced

5 cups basil leaves (packed)

½ cup of olive oil (if you like it thicker, I SUGGEST YOU USE less olive oil)

10 cranks of the peppercorn grinder

Ingredients For the rest:

2 large sweet potato (each 350g), peeled, Blade C

3 cups of shredded mozzarella (it is optional)

4 cups of small broccoli florets

Pepper, to taste

2/3 cup of low-sodium vegetable broth

Directions:

1. Meanwhile, you heat the oven to a temperature of 400 degrees.
2. After which you place all of the ingredients for the pesto into a food processor and pulse until smooth.
3. After that, you taste and just, if necessary.
4. At this point, you pour half of the pesto out into a bowl and add in the broccoli.
5. Then you toss until broccoli is coated with the pesto.
6. Furthermore, you set the broccoli and remaining pesto aside.
7. Then in the bottom of the casserole, you spread out a thin layer of pesto.
8. After that, you spread out a layer of the sweet potato rice and then, add the broccoli.
9. This is when you add the rest of the rice to cover the broccoli and then drizzle the remaining pesto over the rice.
10. In addition, you pour over the vegetable broth and season with pepper.
11. Remember, if you using mozzarella, spread over in an even layer over the rice to cover.
12. Finally, you cover the casserole with tinfoil and bake for 40 minutes.

Nutritional value:

Amount per serving: 1 serving size

Calories: 168

Fat: 12.9g

Carbohydrate: 10.7g

Dietary fiber: 1.3g

Protein: 4.6g

Garlic Sweet Potato Rice

Ingredients

2 tablespoons of olive oil

1 cup of chicken broth (low-sodium)

2 large sweet potato (about 320g+), peeled, Blade C

2 large garlic clove (minced)

Salt and pepper (to taste)

Directions:

1. First, you place your sweet potato noodles into a food processor and pulse until made into rice-like "bits." Then you set aside.
2. After which you add in the olive oil in a large skillet.
3. As soon as the oil heats, you add in the garlic and cook for about 30 seconds.
4. After that, you add in the sweet potato bits and season with salt and pepper.
5. This is when you stir to combine thoroughly and let cook for about 3 minutes, tossing frequently.
6. Finally, you add in the chicken broth and let reduce, about 3-4 minutes.
7. At this point, you taste and add more broth to reduce, if needed.
8. Then when it is done, plate and enjoy alongside your meal!

Nutritional value:

Amount per serving: 1 serving size

Calories: 168

Fat: 12.9g

Carbohydrate: 10.7g

Dietary fiber: 1.3g

Protein: 4.6g

Butternut Squash Mac and Cheese

Ingredients

Olive oil cooking spray

2 tablespoons of coconut flour

½ cup of grated parmesan cheese

2 butternut squash (peeled, Blade B)

4 tablespoons of vegan butter

2/3 cup of plain almond milk

1 cup of grated sharp cheddar cheese

Directions:

1. Meanwhile, you heat the oven to a temperature of 400 degrees.
2. After which you take your spiralized butternut squash noodles and cut with a scissor, if they are not in half-moon shape.
3. After that, you lay the noodles on a baking tray coated in cooking spray.
4. Then you bake in the oven for about 5-7 minutes or until easily pierced with a fork and then set aside.
5. This is when you add in the vegan butter in a large saucepan, and let melt.
6. As soon as it melts, you add in the coconut flour and whisk together until flour absorbs butter and becomes thick.
7. Furthermore, you add in the almond milk and whisk together constantly until mixture thickens.
8. As soon as the mixture thickens, you add in the baked butternut squash noodles and stir to combine and once combined, add in the cheese and stir again to combine.
9. However, if it is too thick, I suggest you add in more almond milk.
10. Finally, once the cheeses have melted into the noodles and consistency is to your preference, you divide into bowls and enjoy!

Nutritional value:

Amount per serving: 1 serving size

Calories: 168

Fat: 12.9g

Carbohydrate: 10.7g

Dietary fiber: 1.3g

Protein: 4.6g

Spicy Garlic Lump Crab Butternut Squash Pasta with Feta & Parsley

Ingredients

2 butternut squash (peeled, Blade C)

½ cup of olive oil

½ teaspoon of red pepper flakes

2 tablespoons of freshly chopped parsley

Olive oil (to drizzle)

Salt and pepper (to taste)

2 garlic clove (minced)

1 ½ cup of lump crab meat

½ cup of crumbled feta

Directions:

1. Meanwhile, you heat the oven to a temperature of 400 degrees.
2. After which you spread out the butternut squash noodles in a baking tray.
3. After that, you drizzle lightly with olive oil and season with salt and pepper.
4. As soon as the oven preheats, you add in the butternut squash noodles.
5. Then you cook for about 7-10 minutes or until softened.
6. At this point, you add in the olive oil in a large skillet.
7. As soon as the oil heats, you add in the garlic and cook for about 30 seconds and then, add in the red pepper flakes and crab meat.
8. Furthermore, you cook, stirring frequently, for about 3 minutes or until the crab meat is heated.
9. Then you place the butternut squash noodles in a bowl and pour in crab meat mixture.
10. Finally, you top with parsley and feta.
11. Enjoy!

Nutritional value:

Amount per serving: 1 serving size

Calories: 168

Fat: 12.9g

Carbohydrate: 10.7g

Dietary fiber: 1.3g

Protein: 4.6g

Roasted Butternut Squash Noodles & Quinoa with Spiced Pumpkin Seeds, Dried Cranberries and Goat Cheese

Ingredients

4 tablespoons of dried cranberries

2 tablespoons of chili powder

2 tablespoons of cumin

2 tablespoons of olive oil

Olive oil cooking spray

(2) 3" piece of butternut squash (peeled, Blade C)

2 tablespoons of raw hulled pumpkin seeds

2 tablespoons of cooked red quinoa

Salt and pepper

4 tablespoons of crumbled goat cheese

Directions:

1. Meanwhile, you heat the oven to a temperature of 375 degrees.
2. After which you cook the quinoa according to package instructions and then set aside when done.
3. Furthermore, while the quinoa is cooking, you coat a baking tray with cooking spray and spread out the pumpkin seeds.
4. After that, you coat the pumpkin seeds with cooking spray and season generously with salt.
5. At this point, you dust the seeds evenly with the cumin and chili powder.
6. Then you bake the pumpkin seeds for about 5 minutes in the oven and when you done, set aside.
7. This is when you change the heat on the oven to a temperature of 400 degrees.
8. In addition, you add the butternut squash noodles onto a baking tray coating with cooking spray.
9. After which you drizzle half of the olive oil onto the noodles and toss to combine.
10. After that, you season with salt and pepper and bake for about 5-7 minutes or until noodles have softened to your preference.
11. Then you place the noodles in a bowl and toss with cranberries, spiced pumpkin seeds, quinoa, and the rest of the olive oil.
12. Finally, you plate onto a bowl and top with goat cheese.
13. Enjoy!

Nutritional value:

Amount per serving: 1 serving size

Calories: 168

Fat: 12.9g

Carbohydrate: 10.7g

Dietary fiber: 1.3g

Protein: 4.6g

Roasted Butternut Squash Zucchini Pasta with Kale, Apricots and Wheat berries

Ingredients

1 cup of cubed butternut squash

4 tablespoons of wheat berries

2 cups of kale

2 small garlic clove (minced)

2 tablespoons of grated Parmigiano-Reggiano cheese (feel free to add more for garnish)

2 large zucchini (Blade C)

2 tablespoons of olive oil (feel free to add more for drizzling)

2 cups of water

8 apricots (roughly chopped)

Salt and pepper (to taste)

Directions:

1. Meanwhile, you heat the oven to a temperature of 405 degrees.
2. After which you add in the butternut squash on a baking tray.
3. After that, you drizzle lightly with olive oil and mix to combine.
4. At this point, you season with salt and pepper.
5. Then you bake the butternut squash for about 25 minutes.
6. Furthermore, while the butternut squash is cooking, you bring 2 cups of water to a boil.
7. As soon as the water boils, you add in the wheat berries, bring to a boil again and then let simmer for about 15 minutes or until the wheat berries are fluffy and the water has evaporated.
8. After which you set aside once done.
9. Then about 5 minutes before the butternut squash is done roasting, place a large skillet over medium heat.
10. This is when you add in the tablespoons of olive oil.
11. As soon as the oil heats, you add in the garlic and cook for 1 minute.
12. In addition, you add in the kale, season with salt and pepper, and cook for about 2 minutes or until the kale is mostly wilted.
13. Then you add in the zucchini noodles, season with pepper, and cook for about 2 minutes or until zucchini softens.
14. After which you add in the cheese, apricots and stir to combine.
15. At this point, you cook for another minute and then plate into a bowl.
16. Finally, you top with wheat berries, butternut squash and garnish with additional cheese and enjoy!

Nutritional value:

Amount per serving: 1 serving size

Calories: 168

Fat: 12.9g

Carbohydrate: 10.7g

Dietary fiber: 1.3g

Protein: 4.6g

Zucchini Rice with Cranberries, Bacon, Goat Cheese and Walnuts with Maple-Dijon Dressing

Ingredients

8 strips of bacon

2 oz. of crumbled goat cheese

2 medium to large zucchini (Blade C)

½ cup of dried cranberries

2/3 cup of coarsely chopped walnuts

Ingredients For the dressing:

1 tablespoon of extra virgin olive oil

3 tablespoons of maple syrup

3 tablespoons of apple cider vinegar

1 ½ teaspoon of whole grain Dijon mustard

Salt and pepper (to taste)

Directions:

1. First, you place the zucchini noodles in a food processor and pulse until rice-like, being careful not to over-pulse, as the zucchini will turn to mush.
2. After which, you set the zucchini rice into a colander and let drip into a sink or bowl while you continue with the rest of the recipe.
3. After that, you place a large non-skillet over medium heat.
4. At a point, when skillet heats, you add in the bacon and cook for about 5-7 minutes until crispy, flipping halfway.
5. Furthermore, you set aside on a paper towel lined plate.
6. After that, you combine all of the ingredients for the maple-Dijon dressing into a small bowl or dressing shaker and whisk together then set aside.
7. This is when you pour the zucchini rice into a large mixing bowl and press down with paper towels to absorb any leftover excess moisture.
8. Then you add in the walnuts, cranberries, goat cheese and crumble in the bacon.
9. Finally, you pour over the dressing and toss to combine.

Nutritional value:

Amount per serving: 2.0 serving

Calories: 346

Fat: 23g

Carbohydrate: 31g

Dietary fiber: 4g

Protein: 10g

Greek Zucchini "Orzo" Salad

Ingredients

Ingredients For the salad:

1 cup of halved pitted Kalamata olives

2 cups of canned artichoke hearts (drained and quartered)

½ cup of diced red onion

3 cups of seeded and chopped roma tomatoes

2/3 cup of crumbled feta cheese

2 cups of baby spinach

Ingredients For the dressing:

2 tablespoons of extra virgin olive oil

4 tablespoons of lemon juice

½ teaspoon of dried parsley

Pepper (to taste)

3 tablespoons of red wine vinegar

2 teaspoon of Dijon mustard

½ teaspoon of dried oregano

½ teaspoon of dried basil

Ingredients For the orzo:

3-4 medium zucchinis (Blade C/D)

Directions:

1. First, you place the zucchini noodles into a food processor and pulse until orzo-shaped (like a longer rice.) make sure it is done carefully not to over-pulse, as zucchini is moist and will become mushy.
2. After that, you pat dry and set aside.
3. At this point, you combine all of the ingredients for the dressing into a bowl and whisk together.
4. This is when you taste and adjust to your preference.
5. Furthermore, you place all of the ingredients for the salad along with the zucchini in a large mixing bowl and pour over the dressing.

6. After which you toss thoroughly to combine and serve or save in the refrigerator for up to 4 days for maximum freshness.

Nutritional value:

Amount per serving: 1 serving size

Calories: 168

Fat: 12.9g

Carbohydrate: 10.7g

Dietary fiber: 1.3g

Protein: 4.6g

Al Fresco Zucchini Pasta Salad

Ingredients

1.5 cups of fresh broccoli flowerets

1 medium yellow bell pepper (diced)

2 tablespoons of extra virgin olive oil

1 teaspoon of Dijon mustard

1 (28 ounce) can Tuttorosso Diced Tomatoes in rich tomato juice (drained)

3 medium zucchini (spiralized, noodles trimmed)

1 large carrot (spiralized using Blade C, noodles trimmed)

¼ cup of white wine vinegar

1 teaspoon of Italian seasoning

Salt and black pepper (to taste)

⅛ Teaspoon of garlic powder

Directions:

1. First, you bring a large saucepan filled halfway with water and a pinch of salt to a boil.
2. After which you add broccoli and carrots and cook for about 3 minutes; drain and rinse with cold water to stop cooking.
3. After that, you combine the vinegar, Italian seasoning, olive oil, salt, mustard, black pepper and garlic power in a screw top jar.
4. Then you cover and shake well.
5. Furthermore, you combine the broccoli, zucchini noodles, carrots, diced tomatoes and yellow bell pepper in a large bowl.
6. Finally, you shake dressing and pour over zucchini pasta mixture; toss gently to coat.

Nutritional value:

Amount per serving: 6.0 serving

Calories: 111

Fat: 5g

Carbohydrate: 14g

Dietary fiber: 4g

Protein: 4g

Raw Coconut-Mango Zucchini Noodles with Cashews

Ingredients

Ingredients For the noodles:

1 ½ cups of roughly chopped raw cashews

3 tablespoons of unsweetened coconut flakes (I prefer Bob's Red Mill Unsweetened Coconut Flakes)

6 medium-to-large zucchinis (Blade C, noodles trimmed)

2 cup of cubed mango

Ingredients For the dressing:

½ cup of freshly squeezed lime juice

Salt and pepper (to taste)

2 cans of full-fat coconut milk, refrigerated overnight or stored without shaking

Flesh from 2 avocados

Directions:

1. First, you open the can of coconut milk and carefully scoop out a half of a cup of the creamy top portion of the coconut milk.
2. After which you reserve the rest of the can for future use or discard.
3. After that, you add that half cup into a food processor, along with the rest of the ingredients for the dressing.
4. Then you pulse until creamy.
5. At this point, you taste and adjust to your preferences.
6. This is when you toss together the zucchini noodles with the dressing in a large mixing bowl, until the noodles are completely coated in the dressing.
7. Finally, you fold in the cashews and mangoes and toss again.
8. Then you divide onto plates and garnish with about 2 teaspoons of coconut flakes per plate.

Nutritional value:

Amount per serving: 4.0 serving

Calories: 380

Fat: 30g

Carbohydrate: 23g

Dietary fiber: 8g

Protein: 8g

Thai Quinoa and Zucchini Noodle Salad

Ingredients

Ingredients For the salad:

2 large carrot, peeled, Blade C, noodles trimmed (or better still julienned)

1 cup of diced green onions

½ packed cup of fresh cilantro

4 medium zucchinis (peeled, Blade C, noodles trimmed)

2 large bell pepper (sliced thinly)

2 cups of cooked quinoa (I prefer red)

4 tablespoons of slivered raw almonds

Ingredients For the dressing:

3 tablespoons of lime juice

2 tablespoons of soy sauce (or better still tamari, if gluten-free)

1 tablespoons of honey

4 tablespoons of water, to thin (or better still more as needed)

½ cup of almond butter

2 tablespoons of rice wine vinegar

1 tablespoon of sesame oil

2 teaspoons of grated fresh ginger

1 tablespoon of sriracha (or preferably other Asian hot sauce)

Directions:

1. First, you place all of the ingredients for the dressing into a food processor and pulse until creamy – or simply whisk together thoroughly.
2. After which you taste and adjust, if necessary then set aside.
3. After that, you place the zucchini noodles in a large mixing bowl along with the carrot, green onions, bell pepper, almonds, quinoa and cilantro.
4. At this point, you pour the dressing over the salad and toss together thoroughly.
5. Finally, you transfer the salad to a serving bowl and enjoy.

Nutritional value:

Amount per serving: 4.0 serving

Calories: 350

Fat: 15g

Carbohydrate: 45g

Dietary fiber: 6g

Protein: 11g

Summer Zucchini Pasta Salad with Greek Yogurt-Herb Dressing

Ingredients

Salt (to taste)

2 (14oz) can chickpeas, drained, rinsed

4 medium zucchinis

4 medium ears of yellow corn, husked

2 cups of grape tomatoes (quartered and seeds squeezed out)

1 cup of small diced red onion

2 large basil chiffonade (2 handful of ribbon-sliced basil)

Ingredients For the dressing:

4 tablespoons of sherry vinegar

2 teaspoons of lemon juice

2 tablespoons of finely minced parsley

Pepper (to taste)

2 cloves of garlic (very finely minced)

½ cup of plain nonfat Greek yogurt

½ teaspoon of onion salt

2 teaspoons of extra virgin olive oil

Directions:

1. First, you place all of the ingredients for the dressing in a bowl and whisk together.
2. After which you set aside in the refrigerator.
3. After that, you place the corn in a pot and cover with water.
4. This is when you lightly salt the water and bring to a boil.
5. As soon as it starts boiling, let cook for about 2 more minutes or until corn is easily pierced with a fork.
6. At this point, you drain into a colander and shave the kernels off the corn with a knife and set aside.
7. Furthermore, you slice the zucchinis halfway lengthwise, careful not to pierce the center.
8. After that you spiraled, using Blade B and place in a bowl with the beans, tomatoes, corn, onion and basil.
9. Finally, you pour over the dressing and toss to thoroughly combine.

Nutritional value:

Amount per serving: 5.0 serving

Calories: 183

Fat: 2g

Carbohydrate: 34g

Dietary fiber: 7g

Protein: 9g

Spiralized Sushi Bowl with Salmon Sashimi and Ginger Miso Dressing

Ingredients

2 large cucumber (Blade C, noodles trimmed)

2 sheet nori (dried seaweed), thinly sliced

avocado (insides sliced)

10 teaspoons toasted white sesame seeds

2 large daikon radish (peeled, Blade C)

2 large carrot (Blade C, noodles trimmed)

24 oz. salmon sashimi (or preferably kani, or tofu, or anything you'd like!)

8 scallion stalks (chopped)

Ingredients For the dressing:

8 tablespoons of apple cider vinegar

2 tablespoons of soy sauce, low sodium

4 tablespoons of tahini

4 teaspoons of grated ginger

4 teaspoons of miso paste

4 teaspoons of honey

Directions:

1. First, you place the daikon noodles into a food processor and pulse until rice-like.
2. After which you squeeze the excess moisture out of the daikon "rice" then set aside.
3. After that, you whisk together all of the ingredients for the dressing until creamy in a medium bowl.
4. Feel free to use a food processor if need be.
5. If you want to assemble:
6. First, you place even amounts of the daikon rice into bowls and top with even amounts of carrot, avocado, salmon sashimi, cucumber, scallions and sesame seeds.
7. Then you top each with dressing and serve.

Nutritional value:

Amount per serving: 1 serving size

Calories: 168

Fat: 12.9g

Carbohydrate: 10.7g

Dietary fiber: 1.3g

Protein: 4.6g

Basque Chicken with Red Potato Noodles

Ingredients

Salt and pepper (to taste)

1 yellow onion (thinly sliced)

½ teaspoon of paprika

2 cups of grape tomatoes (roughly chopped, seeds discarded)

1 cup of chicken broth (low sodium)

1 teaspoon of fresh thyme

3 tablespoons of freshly minced parsley (to garnish)

2 lb. skinless, boneless chicken thighs or breasts (cut into 2" pieces)

1 tablespoon of extra virgin olive oil

2 small red bell pepper (thinly sliced into strips)

2 garlic clove (minced)

2 large red potato (Blade C)

½ teaspoon of red pepper flakes

1 cup of small pimiento-stuffed olives (about 8)

Directions:

1. First, you season the chicken with salt and pepper.
2. After which you heat the oil in a large Dutch oven or deep skillet, over medium-high.
3. After that, you add in the chicken and cook for about 5 minutes or until lightly browned, turning occasionally to evenly cook.
4. Then you add in the onion, pepper, paprika and cooking 2-3 minutes or until crisp-tender.
5. At this point, you add in the garlic, red pepper flakes, broth, tomatoes, thyme and season with salt.
6. This is when you bring to a boil and then reduce heat to a simmer, cooking covered for about 5 minutes and then uncover, add in the potato noodles, toss to combine evenly and then cook for another 10 minutes or until chicken is tender and potato noodles are cooked through.
7. Furthermore, you stir in the olives, garnish with parsley and serve.
8. Finally, you transfer to a cast-iron skillet for presentation, but you can divide immediately into plates or serve in the Dutch oven/pot.

Nutritional value:

Amount per serving: 1 serving size

Calories: 168

Fat: 12.9g

Carbohydrate: 10.7g

Dietary fiber: 1.3g

Protein: 4.6g

Conclusion

To lose weight is very easy if you know the process and how to go about it. That is the reason for this Book, to help you achieve your weight loss goal in No time. Get in shape while eating the foods you love. Take advantage of this top new healthy and delicious spiralizer recipes provided for you in this book.

Remember, the only bad action you can take is no action at all.

www.ingramcontent.com/pod-product-compliance
Lightning Source LLC
Chambersburg PA
CBHW081729100526
44591CB00016B/2552